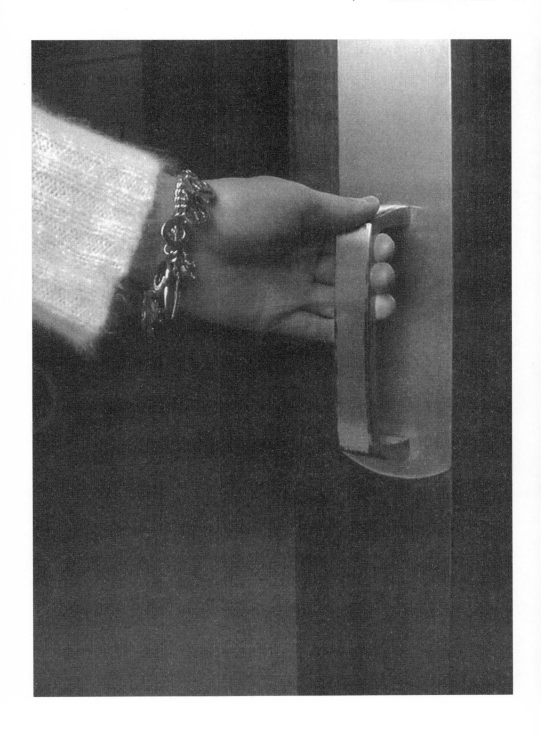

Up my steps, and through my doors,
down my halls, across my floors,
seems to me we've met before -
so, *welcome!* once again.

Was I, for you, a source of pride?
A place where you felt safe inside?
One with the world's doors open wide?
I hope I was, my friend.

And now that you've returned to me,
- if even temporarily -
I hope, for you, fond memories,
as you remember when.

In memory of those playground girls
who seemed too shy to speak.
The same ones who'd out-skip us all
with rocks down at the creek.
And 'specially to one brown-eyed miss
with wings upon her feet,
who somehow caught me, pinned me down,
and kissed me on the cheek.

And also to my mom and dad ...
'best teachers that I ever had.

Hartwell Publications
5290 Cedar Way Drive N.E.
Corydon, Indiana 47112
1-812-952-3482
E-mail: 8oclock@aye.net

Great appreciation is extended for the photographic contributions of:
The Special Collections Division of the University of Louisville
Photographic Archives, The New Albany High School Archives and The
Hazelwood Junior High School Archives, New Albany, Indiana,
Kyle Brewer, Jerry Cook, Jim Brewer, Irvin Goldstein, Ron Shaw,
Connie Hodges, Harmon Bidwell and Wade Bell.
Special thanks, and all my love to Vicki, Allison, and Jennifer,
and thanks, as well, to Tina Houser, Charles Moman, Jim Hodges, David
Kaiser, Lee Cable, Jim Kendall, Kerri Cokeley, Brian Brewer, Scott Brewer,
Alan South, Steve Uesseler, Tanner Cook, Rusty Denison, John Seville,
Selma Dempster, Susan Freiberger, Libby Freiberger,
Robert Wagner, and American Thermos L.L.C.

Live performances of these verses and
their accompanying music are presented by the author.
For inquiries concerning a reading
for students, teachers and others, visit

www.booksbybrewer.com

The
8 O'Clock Bell

Neil Brewer

Introduction

An introduction to *school?* Certainly, no one beyond the age of *six* really needs such a thing, but the verses within may well stand as a *re*-introduction to a world of experiences and their associated feelings which may not be tucked quite as far away as we might think. And no matter *where*, or *when* we attended school, many of these experiences and feelings bring us together.

For from its most harrowing bullified nightmares to its most passionate after-the-ballgame dances, from the depths of its most disappointing report cards to its highest peaks of hilarity, *school has been these things*, or at least some storied *piece* of these things, to all of us at one time or another.

Several of the photographs included in this book were taken in schools nearly a hundred years ago, yet they clearly point out to us that, in many ways, school hasn't dramatically changed since the pencil. Perhaps the styles of the clothes were a little different, or the desks had inkwells - *but look to the eyes!*

The excitement, wonder, anger, anticipation, worry, humor, love and frustration associated with school is seen on the faces of schoolkids (and teachers) from *any* era. Thus, this collection of verses rings true for virtually anyone who ever had a lunch money envelope pinned to his or her chest.

Part One: *Of Teachers and Teaching*, came into existence through my own teaching for the past quarter century, and anyone who has ever taught kids of any grade level will have lived out many a line in these sometimes humorous, sometimes rather reflective verses.

But, no matter what your occupation, you will no doubt find yourself (or someone you knew) within Part Two: *Of Classmates and Class.* From the class clowns, to those who took the idea of a schoolhouse education a bit more seriously, they're all here. Of course, their *names* may be different, but that doesn't matter.

You know who they really were.

Contents

Part One:

Of Teachers and Teaching

Part Two:

Of Classmates and Class

Well, *here I am* Miss Hutchison! You said to *hurry back!*
I found you something special, and I brought him in this sack.
The year has only started, but *already* I can tell -
you'll *always* be my favorite!
(And I *like* the way you *smell*.)

I told my mother what you said,
and *she* said, *"That's* for sure!"
But - have you *really never* seen a kid like *me* before?

Part One

Of
Teachers
and Teaching

Persevere

When teaching takes us for a ride
with children hard to steer,
God grant us strength and courage,
and the faith to persevere.

When common sense, and caring, too,
have all but disappeared,
God grant us strength and courage,
and the faith to persevere.

When great responsibilities
bring to us times of tears,
God grant us strength and courage,
and the faith to persevere.

Oh! That we'll hang on to our sense
of humor through the years,
God grant us strength and courage,
and the faith to persevere.

For finally, when there at the door,
their faces reappear -
we'll know what efforts made were for,
and why we persevered.

A Parent's Brightness

Not unlike a distant star,
a *child's* light may appear small.
So, 'til we have traveled the distance between,
we've not *really* seen either's at all.

And if we dare to *make* such trips,
the chances are we'll find,
two lights once thought to be so faint -
quite brilliant all the time.

Through Them

You could've been an *architect,*
and spanned the widest rivers.
You could've been a *surgeon*,
one who transplants hearts and livers.
You could've *ridden rockets -*
been the first soul off to Mars!
You could've *filled* the concert halls,
and lived among the stars.
A *world* of occupations led
to fame, and lots of cash,
but *you* selected something
that meant *more* to you than that.
Through *them,* you'll see your bridges built;
you'll learn of lives they change.
Through them, you will explore,
and hear the music they arrange.
So, when you dwell upon the thoughts
of things you *might've* done ...
rest well, and know you'll do them *all -*
through those whom *they* become.

As Children

As children, we found wonders hiding
'neath the leaf and stone.
But as adults, we usually find them
better left alone.

Again though, might we grasp a rock,
and slow our pace to know it!
If not to realize the Earth,
to wind up hard -
and throw it.

Great Teachers

Because we love to share,
we have a natural sense of pride -
which often makes it tough to stop,
and set ourselves aside.

And though we often feel the need
to keep our jaws a-flappin,
true learning is discovery -
and the great ones let it happen.

Robbie Parks

When *I* recall class, from my long-ago past,
I think of Rob Parks and his problem.
He'd fight with the boys, or in class he'd make noise,
and Mrs. Rue had no clue how to stop him.

Rob's hands were the tools that he used to break rules.
They were constantly waving or tapping.
And poor Mrs. Rue, said they *kept* tapping, too,
when the rest of us took time for napping.

Well, things only got worse, 'til one day, from her purse,
Mrs. Rue pulled out Robbie a present.
When we saw it, we gasped, "No! You can't give him *that!*"
But for some reason, Rob seemed so pleasant.

Just as if *we* weren't there, Robbie rapped on his snare,
but he paused after playing a while.
And still, to this day, each who sat there would say,
that was when we first saw Robbie smile.

So, how *far* did Rob get? To a New York quartet.
And he calls Mrs. Rue now and then.
And he plays o'er the phone, as she listens alone,
bringin' smiles to each other again.

Ridiculous Plays

Very well, I recall that ridiculous play.
Kids painting scenery in class every day.
The whole schedule suffered, my plans went astray.
All because I took on that ridiculous play.

I had no *idea* how much work it would take.
And what was it *for?* The few dollars we'd make?
And would *I* be to blame for those silly mistakes
that kids make in ridiculous plays?

Where would I get a costume for every last child?
How would lines be remembered - the girls' hair be styled?
And what part could *John* have? (Because John was wild.)
These the woes of ridiculous plays.

Well somehow, and suddenly, and out of nowhere,
came parents and helpers who had things to share.
And the show took on meaning that before wasn't there,
for that worn out, ridiculous play.

Don't ask how it happened - John got the lead role,
and the crowd sat enthralled as John stole the whole show.
Johnny beamed as his father watched from the fourth row,
on the night of that ridiculous play.

One play a year now. I stand by that rule.
Beyond that, I know I could never refuel.
But, never before had John's dad come to school.

Plenty said, for ridiculous plays.

For Awhile

My mom's not home. My dad's in jail.
My bedroom leaks, and drips in pails.
I guess this place will be ok.
At least it's got some room to play.
The last place didn't have a yard,
but it was all mom could afford.
These days, she's got a better job,
so we moved in with her friend, Rob.
They smoke and drink an awful lot.
(My sis did, too, 'til she got caught.)
They've gone to town and left us here.
We're old enough, so I don't care.
My sister's s'posed to help me work,
but she won't do it - she's a jerk.
She's always talkin' on the phone,
so I'll just do it on my own.
And if my homework makes me cuss,
I'll get the answers on the bus.
And that will make my teacher smile.
And things will be real nice.
Awhile.

Camp

The bugs are out and biting, and the morning air is damp,
which means just one of two things: stay inside, or go to camp.
The kids have counted down the days
since back when school first started.
I feel a rash developing, and we've not yet departed.
But soon enough (as always) I'll be re-psyched up to go,
and hit the great outdoors with eighty-some-odd kids in tow.
We'll brave the stormy weather, for it's surely bound to pour,
and eat our beans and weenies 'til we can't eat any more.
We'll hike the trails both down and up,
and then both up and down,
and never see the circles in which we've all walked around.
But still, these kids will see me as a leader void of fear,
because I'll lead them all *where no man's gone*
(at least not since last year).
The campfire in the evening will reveal young, tired faces,
and finally, we'll sing one last song,
and move to sleeping places.
The lights will be shut down,
and cue the flashlights on the wall.
And after 12 or 13 threats, I'll confiscate them all.
And then it's off to sleep,
while there might still be such a chance,
'cause soon enough, I'll have one sick,
or one who needs new pants.
But most will make it through the night
to meet dawn's new discoveries,
and by the second evening, I'll look forward to recovery.
But just as always, I'll survive, with playful moans about it,
while knowing all along, that I'd not have kids be without it.
For if my class curriculum should ever need revamping,
without a doubt, the *last* to go,
would be our springtime camping.

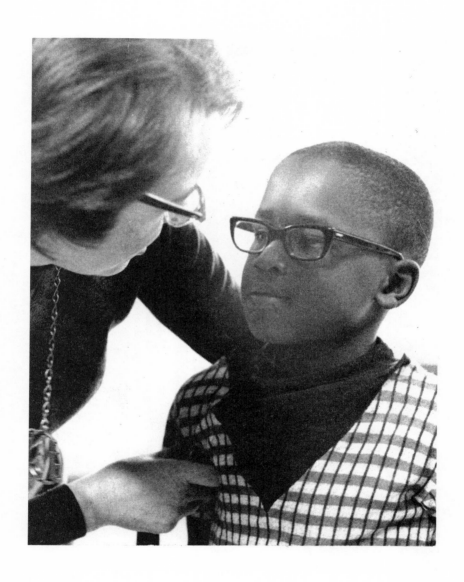

How to Teach

There's the phone!
It's probably a parent for a child.
I've got two running temperatures,
and one is running wild.

Another one's still sniffling
from the tears he cried at lunch.
He doesn't know who threw the spoon -
I think I've got a hunch.

Another says another took
her favorite ballpoint pen.
But the other says she didn't,
so it's *"here we go again."*

I've got one with a paper cut
requiring quick attention,
and now back to the wild one -
he just earned himself detention.

There goes another to the nurse,
she's checking heads for lice.
And now one with a scratch
thinks he should go down for some ice.

This math class isn't over yet -
we've still got 15 minutes.
We won't get finished what we should,
but, maybe we'll begin it.

I think that Teacher College
ought to add some new instruction,
and call it: *How To Teach -
With Never-Ending Interruptions!*

Hurry Up!

We rush kids into reading, and we rush kids into math.
We rush kids into thinking they need more of this and that.
Whatever be the reason we make being young complex,
it only makes me wonder what we'll rush kids into next.

My Ducks in a Row

I'm teaching the test, and forgettin' the rest -
'cause somebody, somewhere, thinks that's for the best.

No time for diversions or elsewhere excursions -
what matters the most, is we learn the same versions.

So, it's farewell to free-time, and thoughts that are random -
I'll ready these kids for any test they can hand 'em.

And we'll all be impressed by the things they recite,
the names they recall, and whose words they can write.
And all will be calm - no more movers or shakers -
with the world in the hands of the *expert* test takers.

A Teacher's Dream

Last night I dreamed I died,
and found myself in teacher heaven,
and I could not *believe* the splendid things that I was given!

A simply *perfect* classroom filled with every teaching tool
that I had ever asked for, since I started teaching school.

But all was just a dream, as I found out, when I awakened ...
for with my eyes wide open, each and every one was taken.

Then, suddenly recalling all my lovely teaching gifts -
I realized the ultimate omission from my list.

Why weren't my *children* in my dream?
But then, I understood.
That room was full of *perfect* things -
and kids just aren't that good.

My dreaming had awakened me
to what that stuff was worth ...
and I'd been blessed to see that *kids* are heaven, here on Earth.

Take One! (and *Only* One!)

School's like a movie - a Hollywood feature,
with players to fill every role.
Directing the cast from the wings are the teachers,
and students are stars of the show.

The film includes horror, excitement, and grief -
comedy, anger, and love.
And sometimes a scene is beyond our belief,
because *in* it, are *all* the above!

The picture's a wild combination of sorts -
an epic adventure of firsts.
Some scenes take forever, and some are cut short,
read from scripts that are never rehearsed.

Here's hoping *you* got every part that you wanted -
from crayons, until graduation.
Here's hoping that, too, all your *teachers* came through,
with Academy Award nominations.

Each and Every One

We haven't all starred in the circus,
and we haven't all dressed up in kilts.
We haven't all raced in the Derby,
and we haven't all walked upon stilts.

Not many have climbed up Mount Everest.
Not many have walked on the moon.
Not many have flown for the Navy.
Not many have lived with baboons.

We haven't all picked a pineapple -
we haven't all been where they grow.
We haven't all thrown a good snowball,
for in some places, it never snows.

But still, we have one thing in common -
no exception is found to the rule:
when we find ourselves old,
we'll have *all* often told,
of our days in that place we called *school*.

Part Two

Of
Classmates and Class

This Bus is Incredibly Cold!

This bus is *incredibly* cold ...
I'm stiff as a *90*-year-old!
My blood's below freezin' - my windpipe is wheezin'.
This bus is incredibly cold!

I'm cold as a polar bear's nose,
and the food in my lunchbox is froze.
I checked my dill pickle - it's a jumbo *icicle*.
This bus is incredibly cold!

I can't turn my head in these clothes,
and I can't lift my arms past my nose.
Some kid sat beside me - is it *Joe?* Well, it might be,
but I can't turn my head, *so who knows?*

And this bus is incredibly cold!!
We won't forget *this* when we're old!
And when we're all *geezers,* we'll tell of the *freezer,*
that *we* used to ride down the road.

That *New* Kid

That *new* kid ... I've heard he's a bully.
They say he's where *trouble* begins.
All my friends heard it, too, so it's *bound* to be true,
so I'm keepin' my distance from *him.*

That *new* kid ... he *looks* like a bully.
He stands like a bully does, too.
He eyes you with glances, *I'm* not takin' chances,
'cause that's what they say *bullies* do.

That *new* kid ... I *know* he's a bully -
and the kids that I play with agree.
We all know what we've *heard,* so just pass on the word,
that it's best to just let *that* kid be.

Pi'ture Day

It's pi'ture takin' time again - we *do* this *every* year ...
but *I* don't recognize 'bout *half* my classmates standin' here!
We're decked out like it's *church* day,
but, it's *just* a Thursday morn -
and I *am* <u>*itchin'*</u> in the *worst* way
in these duds I've never worn.
Now ... *could* be that's Kris Smith
(behind those caked on lips and cheeks)
but, thick as *that* stuff looks,
Kris won't be *Kris* again for weeks!
And <u>if</u> that's *Eddie* there down front,
then I've won *me* a dollar -
'cause *he* once bet he'd *never* wear a shirt that had a collar.
And finally, I can *not* believe that Jimmy Martin's sick!
('Cause every year, he gives Jill ears *precisely* at the click.)
So, who's gonna want *this* picture?
I can say, "Not *me!*" for sure,
'cause it won't come *half* close to showin'
the way we <u>*really*</u> were.

The King's Lot

It's where I keep *important* things:
my arrowheads - my Ratfink rings -
my baking soda submarine -
and other stuff like that.
What *kind* of stuff? Well, stuff like *this:*
my NASA coins from Krun Chee Chips -
my cherry-flavored Halloween lips -
and a dime I hammered flat.
Good baseball cards - my stack of gum -
(don't tell, and I *might* give you some)
and crystals that I busted from
some *really* neat-o rocks.
Hey! The teacher's busy - take a peek,
and *have a pencil* (they were cheap),
but, don't touch *nothin' else* I keep
inside my see-gar box!

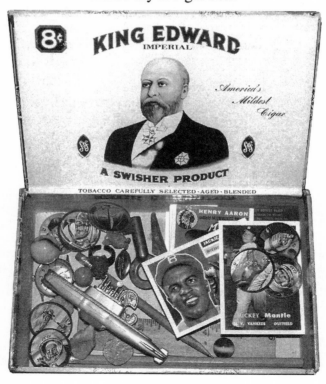

Line Up!

On lunch money day, we would line up to pay.
Every afternoon recess, we lined up to play.
We lined up our desks, and the chairs where we sat.
When the fire alarm rang, we all lined up for *that!*
We lined up for pictures (which most of us hated).
At times, we lined up to be in-oc-u-lated.

We lined up for bathrooms, we lined up for lunches.
In hallways, we walked in a line, *not* in bunches!
On hangers, we lined up our coats and our caps.
In first grade, we laid in straight lines and took naps.
For drills (like tornados) we lined up and sat,
In gym, we lined up for three swings of a bat.

Added up, all those lines would've reached *Oklahoma!*
But - finally, we lined up and got our diplomas.
So, *even in lines,* I guess *we* learned enough -
and maybe our teachers were just toughenin' us up.
For somewhere, in each day of life we *still* find,
that we're waitin' for *somethin'* ... and standin' in line.

Where's Dave?

Dave didn't get on the school bus today.
Last night, I went over to his house to play,
and though he seemed quiet, he still *looked* ok,
but - Dave didn't get on the school bus today.

It might've had somethin' to do with those guys.
They pulled in his driveway wearin' suitcoats and ties.
And one carried somethin' - some kind of surprise.
Yeah - it must've had somethin' to do with those guys.

Hey, I know! A party for Dave's brother, John.
I *know* Dave was *glad* when John left for Viet Nam,
but John's prob'ly back, and *now,* they'll get along.
That's it! A big party for Dave's brother, John.

But that was last night. So where's Dave today?
Boy, he's in *big* trouble, if he's snoozin' away!
I'm sure that his brother's homecomin' was great -
but ... *that* was last night ... *so where's Dave today?*

The Sub

Hoo-ray! We've got a *substitute!*
We'll all pretend we're sweet and cute.
Let's pile up paper wads to shoot,
and have ourselves a blast!
Let's switch our seats, and change our names,
and make her play our favorite games.
In no time flat, we'll have *her* trained.
(We're really good at that!)

But wait - OH, NO!! *It's Mr. <u>Lear</u>!!*
(That *ancient* guy we had *last* year.)
He made us *sit,* and bent our ears,
with stories from his past.
We sat and listened *all day long,*
while he went *on,* and *on,* and *on* ...
repeating himself like a scratchy old song,
from the *first* bell to the *last!*
Miss Jones, *we* know you've got the flu,
and *we* know what we've *put* you through,
but *please,* Miss Jones, we *beg* of you -
come back and save our class!

Cowboy Comic

Kirk Perry was a friend of mine ...
I knew that guy for years,
and he never got enough sleep at night
in his entire school career.
'Cause when teachers gave us homework
for like, math, and other courses,
Kirk stayed up late readin' *comic* books
'bout cowboys and their horses.

Then, on the morning bus, he'd tell us 'bout
that shootin,' ridin' and ropin' -
and *then,* he'd fight the whole day through
just to keep his *eyelids* open.
And sometimes, ol' Kirk's *nose*
wound up all bloodied in a mess -
'cause halfway through a class
his head would **whump!** down on his desk.
The teachers used to say, "Young *man,*
you'll *never* graduate!!"

But he *did* ...
and then he found a *reason* to just keep *on* with stayin' up late.
As a matter of fact, he gets *paid* for that,
'cause he's a third shift city cop.
And at break time, he *still* reads cowboy comics
in the 4th Street Doughnut Shop.

Steve Johnson Pulled the Fire Alarm

Steve Johnson pulled the fire alarm,
and Mr. Higgins knows.
So, Steven's in the office
while *we* freeze our hands and toes.

I hear the sirens comin'
and we had to stop our quiz.
This *building's* not on fire ...
but, I'd bet Steven's *rear-end* is!

Show and Tell

I _loved_ it on "Show and Tell" school days, because
I was flat out the *best* show and teller there was.
Now, *that's* <u>not</u> to say other tellers were *bad,*
but folks chomped at their bits to find out what *I* had.
'Cause, when it came time for *my* turn to begin,
the whole room got *real* quiet, and everybody *leaned* in.
See, they knew that whatever *I'd* brought in *for sure*
was like nothin' they'd seen in a *schoolhouse* before!
Like ...
I *once* brought a box filled with bones - *top to bottom,*
and I *showed* 'em off good. (But didn't *tell* where I got 'em.)
Then I brought in a rat snake, and *they're* worth a <u>mint</u>!
(But the bag had a hole, so who knows where *he* went.)
Still, I'd end *all* my tellin' the very same way:
with a present my grandfather taught me to play.
And though, next to *him,* I don't play all that *well* -
to this day, I still try, 'cause I *still* show and tell.

My Pal, Jody

Jody *always* saves my seat.
I relax when I see the bus turn on my street,
I don't have to hurry, or shove, or compete,
'cause Jody has always been there with my seat.

My old buddy, Jody, will save me a seat.
Our friendship is solid as a slab of concrete.
So, when lunchtime arrives, and we line up to eat,
no problem! I *know* Jody's savin' my seat.

But *what,* Mr. Martin? *What's that you just said?*
Jody's *mom* called? Jody's *sick? - and in bed?!*
My *seat* won't be saved! I'm a goner! *I'm through!*
This life isn't fair!
So ... what *now,* do I do?

46

Miss Brooks

Through mountains of burgers and broccoli spears,
Miss Brooks was the school's cook for 41 years,
and I still see her laugh through those diced onion tears,
as she stirred up that pot full of chili.

Miss Brooks never married. She lived all alone,
and we figured she stayed more at school than at home.
She would constantly tell us all, *we* were her own,
so we thought she was nuts, (but not really).

She could whump up a dinner like you never saw,
and the size of those servings would put you in awe.
Plus, she'd fix us surprises - like chocolate chip balls,
so, we ate like a herd of Paul Bunyons.

Well, same as it always does, time passes by,
and a few days ago, we all heard that she died.
And we gathered, and talked, and we laughed, then we cried
without help from the dicing of onions.

Lunch Time!

My mom packed *me* some carrots,
and *your* mom packed *you* some chips.
My mom packed me an apple,
and *yours* packed *onion dip*!
My mom packed me some *walnuts*
mixed with *raisins* and some *berries* ...
and here, *your* mom packed *Pixie* Stix
and chocolate covered cherries!
I see *you* got a P-B-J.
I thought *I* had one, too.
But, mine was just a *P-B* ...
now my jaws won't come un-glued.
Your mom filled up your thermos - *to the top* - with Upper Ten.
My mom threw in a nickel, so I guess it's *milk* again.
My mom, she went to *college*, so I *know* she learned a bunch ...
but, 'could be, she missed class that day
they learned 'bout fixin' lunch.

Just a Lunchbox

I was somewhere downtown in a store yesterday,
when I came upon lunchboxes there on display,
and a few things I noticed makes it truthful to say
they weren't like any lunchbox *I* had!

First off, *they* were plastic - and *mine* was like steel,
and mine had that smooth, glossy paint kinda' feel ...
but, the *main* thing I noticed, was their *pictures* weren't real,
but *mine* were. (So, I guess *real* is bad!)
'Cause take, for example, *the real Davy Crockett.*
He carried a *gun,* and had a *knife* in his pocket!
So, some wouldn't want *that* box back on the market -
but still, I don't quite understand ...
'cause when *I* was a kid, *we* had shoot-'em-up toys.
Heck, that's just what you *did,* back when *we* were all boys -
but, we knew it was nothin' but after-school *noise,*
and it <u>stopped</u> when our moms called us in.

So, though, *some* might claim there are *pictures* to blame
for a world full of problems too many to name,
I'd say problems like those would be less likely comin',
if *more* parents called ... and more *kids* came a-runnin'.

Recess!

He's safe!!
He's out!!
He's safe!!
He's **out!!**
You don't know what you're *talkin'* about!
Well, you're *goofy,* man, and you're *blind* as a *bat!*
Oh yeah? Well, he's *still* safe on first, and *that's that!*
He's out!!
He's safe!!
He's out!!
He's **safe!!!**
You think if you're *louder*, then you'll get *your* way!!
OK, then - do *over!*
No way, there Jose!!
Well, it's *do-over,* man, or I'm *not* gonna play!!
Oh, no! *There's the whistle!* Time's up! Grab home plate!
Hey - you playin' *tomorrow?*
Heck, yeah! *This is great!!*

Very Impressive

In elementary school ...
I tried impressing Pam by climbing up the monkey bars.
I tried impressing Sue by hanging by my knees for hours.
In junior high ...
I tried impressing Jill by loudly pounding things in shop.
I tried impressing Liz by running track until I dropped.
In high school ...
I tried impressing Lynn by driving 'round in my dad's car.
I tried impressing Jan by kicking footballs high and far.
And when I think of all that
climbing - hanging - pounding -
running - driving - and kicking,
It makes me wonder why ...
I didn't think of trying out a *smile,* and saying, "Hi!"

Playground Show-Off

Everybody, come quick! Danny just did that trick ...
it's the one where he swallows the bark off a stick!
Julie gave him a dime, like she did the last time,
when Dan said that (for ten cents) he'd eat *lemon* rhinds!
He chewed up the rhinds,
and she gave him the dime,
but it doesn't look too good for Danny *this* time.
'Cause he picked up a stick,
and he ate the bark quick,
then the bark turned to barf and now *that* boy is *sick!*

But Danny won't quit - he'll find new things to chew.
It's amazing ... the things money makes people do.

The School Nurse

When we got *hurt* at school, we never knew which was worse:
just lay there and die ... or visit Miss Frakes, the nurse.
You couldn't *truly* say she was "mean as a snake",
'cause they didn't *make* snakes *half* as mean as Miss Frakes.
If you busted your eye, and it swelled and was shinin',
she'd say, "You got <u>two</u>, *so why the heck are <u>you</u> whinin'?"*
You could *run, trip,* and *fall* in a big pile of glass,
and she'd slop on the iodine and scream, "*<u>Back to class!!</u>*"
Billy twisted his neck, and I *heard* it - it *cracked!*
She just grabbed it with both hands, *and twisted it back!*
So now, you know more 'bout Miss Frakes, the school nurse.
(And you *also* know why we *hid* most of our hurts.)

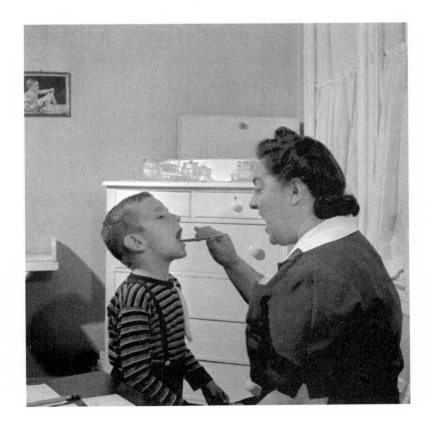

Safety First

They hauled away the monkey bars,
because of Julie Brown.
She bumped her head - her mom called school -
and then they took 'em down.

The *swings* were really first to go,
we lost *them* 'cause of Bruce.
He walked in front of Jenna Smith,
and now his teeth are loose.

We haven't seen the merry-go-round
since Allen smashed his thumb.
His thumb got better *weeks* ago -
but the merry-go-round's still gone.

They've banned us from the seesaw,
and I guess we all know why.
But still, *we* didn't know six *girls*
could *shoot* a boy that high!

So now, we wonder when
they're gonna come and get this slide -
'cause since it's all that's *left* out here,
we're burnin' up our hides.

And if they *do,*
I s'pose we'll just run 'round 'til playtime's passed -
unless they think *that's* unsafe, too,
and dig up all the grass.

The Lovely Miss Monroe

Miss Monroe was lovely ...
like that *movie* star was she,
So, every day, us boys would prove
just how dumb *boys* could be.

She'd laugh ... *we'd* laugh.
She'd teach ... we'd try.
She'd lead ... we'd follow.
She'd smile ... we'd *die!*

She knew she only had to ask,
and we would jump to *any* task.
The girls would watch, their mouths agape,
convinced, I'm sure, boys came from apes.

Us guys were tight - you know the kind,
we swore we'd *never* part.
But Miss Monroe was soon the cause
for each fight we would start.

Then, one day after recess,
she said, "Boys, this *has* to stop!"
That's when we saw her *ring,*
and our whole lives went straight to slop.

Well, up to then the *girls* our age
were lesser lifes than flies,
but now that Miss Monroe was took,
they might be worth a try.

So, our complete attention turned to *one* -
her name was Hester ...
and Miss Monroe *delighted*
in her room of courting jesters.

The Man with a Plan

One day at recess,
clean out of the blue -
Eddie Wilson said,
"That's it! I've *had* it! I'm *through!"*
We stopped with our game,
and big Ronnie Brown said,
"What's za *matta* wit chu?
What chu *talkin'* 'bout Ed?"

But Ed just stared off
in the distance and grinned,
and said, "When that *bell* rings,
I'm *not* goin' in."

"I'm *worn out* with school -
all that *math* and that *writin'*,
I'm worn out with *home,* too -
the *naggin'* and *fightin'*.
I'm gonna hide out
until school *ends* today ...
then I'll come out from hidin'
and just run away!"

Just then, the bell rang -
we all ran to line up,
but, *Ed* wasn't there ...
Ed was <u>gone</u>, sure enough!!

But teachers can sense stuff
(too weird to explain);
it's like they've got *radar*
built into their brains.
In *ten seconds,* they knew
that Ed wasn't around,
Then, in ten or twelve more,
Eddie Wilson was found.

He was up in a tree -
standin' still as a stick.
He was posed like a limb,
but the teachers weren't tricked.
So they made him come down,
and they stood him in line,
and he mumbled and grumbled,
*"They won't find me **next** time!"*

Eddie's plan didn't work,
but he learned a few things:
Don't hide up in *trees* -
at least, *not until Spring!*

The Duchess of Dodge

Look out!! 'Cause *Mary's* got the ball,
and her eyes are set on *you!*
She's lean, she's mean, she's quick and tall -
there's nothin' you can do.

One time, she drew a bead on Fred,
(back when he first moved in).
She slung one straight upside his head!
Fred hasn't played since then.

We laughed when we first saw her throw -
that wind up, fling, and twirl.
Now, every single kid I know,
tries throwin' like that girl.

But, none of us have matched *her* way ...
perhaps it's in the eyes.
We only know that when *she* plays,
we drop like common flies.

When *I* go out into the world,
don't know what job *I'll* do ...
but, I can bet I know *one* girl,
who'll run a *wreckin'* crew!

Bazooka Billy

Watchin' Billy sure was fun,
when he'd cut loose with bubblegum.
He'd bring enough for everyone
and show us how to blow it.

Bill hated school in every way,
except when it was time to play.
He threw *at least* one fit a day,
like only Bill could throw it.

But still, the teachers never ceased
to try and help that Bazooka beast.
But if 'ol Bill cared in the least,
his actions never showed it.

So, *school* can only do so much,
and then the rest is up to us,
and somewhere there's a crazy cuss,
who, these days, prob'ly knows it.

The Girl by the Fence

She didn't *have* clothes like the other ones had.
Their hair was called good, with hers usually called bad,
and I never once stopped to consider how sad
that her days spent in school really were.

It's strange how, these days, that I know we were wrong,
with the chances to "make right" forever now gone.
Still ... sometimes, I find myself dwelling upon
all the things we could've said -
and the things we should've said -
because ...
she *never* had clothes like the other ones had,
and *their* ways were good, with hers usually called bad,
and I doubt I can even imagine how sad
that her days spent in school really were.

Sent Down

She sent me to the office.
Brother! *I* don't know what *for.*
She hollered, "Sit right <u>here</u> young man!!!"
And then she slammed the door.

She's in there with the principal.
I've had it now for sure.
They'll probably even call my mom,
and blab it all to *her!*

Today's my teacher's birthday.
(We found out she's 34.)
And everybody sang, and wished
that she'd have many more.

She didn't like my present -
and I'd raised him from an egg!
But she might like him better,
once he unwinds off her leg.

Holiday Classic

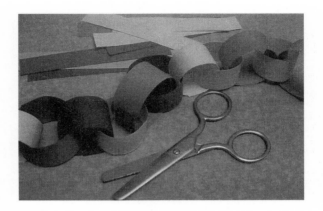

Every year at Christmas time,
we'd get ourselves in groups,
and make those Christmas classics:
paper chains made out of loops.

We *knew* the longest chain
would always win the best reward,
so we fired up assembly lines
just like 'ol Henry Ford.

And then the chain-link race was *on,*
our sites set on the prize,
with visions like those Wright Boys had,
when they set out to fly.

And sometimes, if a link would break,
we weren't *about* to stop!
(Like Thomas Alva didn't,
when those bulbs kept burnin' up.)

So, if some doubters were to say,
"What good was such a lesson?!"
They might do well to think about
those folks who've just been mentioned.

Division

I'm s'posed to count the times
the *left* one goes into the *right,*
and that *right there's* enough
to keep me countin' most the night.

And when I *finally* figure out how many really fits,
it's crazy just how complicated what's *left over* gets.

So, seems to me we'd be best off
if we'd all start believin':
sometimes, the stuff life divvies folks
ain't *s'posed* to come out even!

Teacher's Helper

"Help me out," said Mrs. Burns.
"What grade would *you* give this?"
I said, "An A."
And she said, *"What?!* Count up the ones you *missed!!"*

And so I did, and said, "OK,
perhaps then, it's a B."
She said, "You'd better count *again!!"*
(which meant no B for me.)

And so, *again,* I checked it out,
and said, "I guess a C."
"A *C* would be a *gift* young man!
At *best,* <u>this</u> gets a *D!!"*

And so, of all the teachers I recall, I have no doubt -
that Mrs. Burns remains the one
I *least* liked helping out.

Diary Entry: April 10th

Girls are really goofy.
They think us guys should read their minds.
And then, they get real mad,
'cause we read wrong 'bout half the time.

If they would only tell us
just exactly what they need,
our lives would sure be easier
with one less thing to read.

Diary Entry: April 10th

Guys are really goofy.
It's so weird that they can't see,
that we could make them happy
as a guy could hope to be.

Is doing simple little things
for us so big a task?
We girls could tell them *plenty,*
if they'd ever think to ask.

Tips for Giving a Good Report

Get a plastic cover sheet.
(They make reports look nice and neat.)
And with your paper there inside,
the class will think you're bonafide.
But here's *another* thing or two
that great presenters always do:
comb your hair, and iron your clothes.
Spit out the gum. Don't pick your nose.
And *don't* sit there, thinking, "Ahhhh! *What* could be *worse*?!!"
Stick your *hand* in the air and say, "May I go *first?*"
Such *bold* volunteering will please *any* teacher,
and adds just a touch ... a nice "you went first" feature.
But far more than that, are the *girls* you'll impress,
and that, there alone, makes it worth all the stress.
So take a deep breath, and stand straight and tall,
and whatever you do, don't begin with, *"Hi, Ya'll!"*
And that's about it! But, oh yeah, there's one *more* thing:
be sure that you've written some stuff worth reporting.

The Principal

There seated in his office, wearing stern face, coat and tie,
we knew it from *day one*, this was no *ordinary* guy.
'Cause ordinary guys just couldn't do the things *he* could,
and he didn't have to *prove* 'em, they were outright understood.
If *he* laid down a stare, you'd *swear*
he'd hit you with hypnosis,
and when he walked, we moved aside
like water did for Moses.
His office was the last place in the *world* you'd want to go.
Why? Johnny Stewart *told* us that.
(And he was one who'd know.)
So, we would walk those hallways nothin' less than mortified,
while never really knowin' there was quite a different side.
And it would take us *years* to finally come to realize
that discipline, plus *love,* make extra ordinary guys.

Juicy Fruit Houdini

"JOE WILLIAMS, SPIT THAT **GUM** OUT!!
... *And,* is that <u>all</u> that you have *got?!*"

"Yes Ma'am, it is," Joe'd calmly say.
Joe Williams lied a lot.
'Cause he'd no more spit out a piece,
than one would take its place ...
and you could hardly *tell* it by the look upon his face.

That guy could have a wad of *seven* sticks there in his jaws,
and he could open wide, and you'd *still* not see where it was!

And where he hid his *extra* sticks was just as puzzlin', too.
(He never even told *me,* but he always shared a chew.)

These days, I've heard that Joe is workin' for the FBI,
and *that* job fits him perfectly. I'm sure he's one *great* spy!

'Cause spies don't give stuff 'way by the
expressions on their faces -
and spies don't tell a *soul* about their secret *hidin'* places.

No One Like You

Gayle took lunch money to the office -
gosh, that girl was good with cash ...
meanwhile, *Amanda* did a lovely job of takin' out the trash.
Christina cleaned the chalkboard beautifully -
she'd wipe away the grunge.
(And I must say, she had a way
with that old bucket and a sponge.)
Melinda's mind was so mechanical, and always in a whir -
which made *her* best at diggin' lead
out from the pencil sharpener ...
and *Paula* wonderfully went watering
the plants within their pots,
while *Ellen* vacuumed up the classroom
like she worked for Marriott.
Yes *sir!* Those girls were *fine,*
and they'd *all* do so nicely what they'd do,
but, *not a one* could pound erasers
on the sidewalk same as *you.*
'Cause when you really got to goin', how the chalk dust flew,
but still, you didn't miss a beat until you had 'em lookin' new,
and though some others tried,
you could'a showed 'em all a thing or two,
'cause not a one could pound erasers
on the sidewalk same as you.

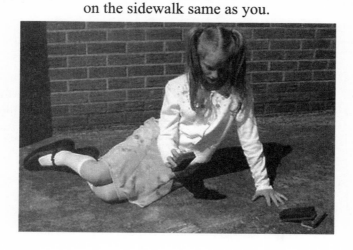

74

Free!

We're FREE! - until each raindrop
from the sky turns into money!
FREE! - until the bees forget the recipe for honey!
FREE! - until the sun burns out, and planet Earth stops turning!
FREE! - until the people who make buttermilk stop churning!
FREE as *Leprechauns* to seek and find each 4-leaf clover!

Well, maybe *not* ...
but still, **we're free**! (... *until the weekend's over!*)

Patrol Duty

Raymond Davis - *that* guy's cool.
He guards this sidewalk after school.
His name is printed on his vest,
right by the words: "Our Future's Best."
His arms go up, and we all stop,
just like we'd do for any cop.

I'd like to get his autograph,
but he's too cool for me to ask.
Heck, *I'm* just in the second grade,
but if I could, I'd be *Ray's* age.

I'd take those sidewalk service vows,
and we would be "Protect-All" pals.
We'd keep our eyes peeled sharp for crimes.
(Like, kids who walked outside the lines.)

But - *there's the whistle!* This day's gone.
Ray's hands have dropped - he's waved us on,
and with the others I walk by,
with hopes that someday he'll say, "Hi."

But Raymond doesn't know I'm here,
and *he'll* start junior high *next* year.
But man, oh man, would *that* be cool -
if, one day, *I'm* a guard at school ...
there, with my vest on every day -
my name *right on it,* next to Ray's.

After School

I remember impressin' just all kinds of folks,
ridin' 'round with those baseball cards stuck to our spokes.
And you *never* saw *any* kids any more proud
than when we wowed a crowd with our spoke-motors loud.
And if Susie was playin' out front in her yard,
then we'd see who was loudest by pedalin' hard.
And we'd *stand* on those pedals and crank it up faster,
but *that* girl - *not once* - even looked when we passed her.
Thinkin' back now, *I'd* bet she was impressed.
(But, a grade-school-age girl just won't show it, I guess.)
Anyway ... when our engines got flimsy, or tore,
we just ripped *that* set off there and slapped on some *more!*
Then, off down the street with our bubblegum smackin'
we'd fly once again with cards clickin' and clackin'.
And though that bike's gone now ... *that's* a loss I can handle,
but, I still sometimes cry 'bout those rookie year Mantles.

Diggin' a Hole

I'm diggin' a hole, yes, I'm diggin' a hole,
and gettin' it dug really *quick* is my goal.
In a few minutes more, mom and dad will be home,
so I'm diggin' a really quick, really big hole.

And down in this hole my report card will go ...
then I'll cover it up so nobody will know.
And then, I suppose, I'll be *finished* with holes.
(At least ... for another good *six weeks* or so.)

The 8 O'Clock Bell

The flapping of the rubber
on the doors upon the bus;
the voices of the bullies
who found constant need to cuss.

The laughter of the friends
who were alike in perfect ways;
the sobs of kindergartners
on their first and second day.

The rattle of a lunchbox
being shoved up on a shelf;
the silence of the kid
who always kept things to himself.

The unzip of the zippers
on the raincoats and the boots;
the sniffling of the sniffers
who used sleeves to wipe their snoots.

The buzz of talking in the halls,
the slam of locker doors;
the sliding scrape of hard-soled shoes
on newly waxed tile floors.

The grind of metal gears
to make a brand new pencil shorter;
the call to, "Bring lunch money up!"
The stacking up of quarters.

The gurgling of the bubbles
keeping fish somewhat alive;
the pounding of erasers
on the concrete steps outside.

The plopping down of books,
and then, the flipping through of pages;
the squeaking of the wheels
when run by hamsters in their cages.

The painful screech of new chalk
grating slowly 'cross the board;
the stirring in of water
when the powdered paint was poured.

The wadding up of papers
after making our mistakes;
the clicking and the clacking
only *film* projectors make.

The tapping of a pencil
on a chair leg or a desk;
the "Shush up!!" "Quiet!!" "Do *NOT* talk!!"
when it was time for tests.

All sounds of vivid memories,
deep within us, tightly locked -
for *each* of us have answered
to the bell at 8 o'clock.

Steven Meyer

Steve Meyer was known as the "Prince of the Paddle",
a *master* of tabletop talents.
His heavy and cumbersome leg brace would rattle,
yet, *no one* could catch him off balance.

Still, it wasn't that way when he *first* came to play;
he was always so *easy* to beat.
But he practiced at home, in his basement alone,
with a burning desire to compete.

You see, Steven's disease made him weak in the knees,
and he couldn't play "run-around" sports.
And no matter how hot, that an August day got,
you'd just *never* catch Steve wearin' shorts.

But weakness aside, that kid's strength came from pride
in the one thing he learned how to ace.
For when challengers came to the one they thought lame,
shortly after, *Steve* showed 'em their place!

Yup, to think of the way Steven Meyer could play
through the patience he took to adjust -
makes me truly believe, that for people like Steve,
the most highest of hurdles are *us*.

What's he doin' *these* days? That - I really can't say,
but I say *this* without apprehension,
that *whatever* it is, I'm sure Steven's a wiz,
with his talents commanding attention.

Music Class

Teacher called me a singer -
a *soaring* humdinger -
a "lover of song" in the chorus,
'cause I'd stand with the gang,
and I beautifully sang
every tune that she laid out before us.

But, it's time to confess
that my voice was a mess,
shootin' up - and then down - like a yoyo.

So then, how did I *do* it?
I just *lipped* my way through it,
and stayed home when she took grades for solos.

Love Note

Kate sat three rows in front of me,
and what a sight was Kate to see.
My life at school would be divine,
if Kate would say that she'd be mine.

I made my note's instructions clear:
"Choose one letter, then send back here."

A of course, was next to "Love you."
B meant "Like you as a friend."
C "I'm going with another."
D "Don't *ever* write again!"

Well, faster than I'd *ever* dreamed,
my note came sailing back to me.
Kate made her answer plain to see ...
she'd filled *both* sides with great big *Ds*.

But *me,* a *quitter?* Hey - *no way!*
And finally, one day, Kate checked <u>A</u>.
And now, we've raised a couple kids,
who tell their mom they're *glad* she did.

Floyd Wilkerson

Floyd Wilkerson, the janitor? Most thought that he was crazy.
He was old, he limped, his voice was gruff,
and one eye looked *real* hazy.
And what he wore ... well,
there's no *way* to say that you'd admire it.
(Fact is, if you'd thrown a parrot in,
Floyd could'a been a *pirate.)*
But, looks can be deceiving - I'm not *sure* who said that first -
but, they were *right,* 'cause Floyd was great!
(Though, now and then, he'd curse.)
Still, what was *great* about him, was he really liked us kids,
and he taught us 'bout as much stuff as 'bout any *teacher* did.
Like, how to use a push broom - 'cause there is a special way,
and how to squeegee windows, so they'd dry up clear as day.
One time he asked me, *"Can you mop?"*
And I said, "Well, heck *yes!"*
And then I 'bout quadrupled what was once a minor mess.
But, Floyd had him a sayin'.
He'd say, *"Learn* from things gone bad!"
Floyd didn't seem to have too much,
but *patience,* that guy had.
Well, turned out it was *years* -
way after Floyd had gone and died,
that we found out just *why* he limped, and had that hazy eye.
It seems he took a trip with friends to France in '44,
and after that, Floyd Wilkerson was changed for evermore.

He lived through troubled times for sure, just like so many did.
But, he never *griped* about it ... leastways, never to us kids.
And though, *some* say that old folks
are just somethin' to avoid ...
I never do.
'Cause someday, *I might find another Floyd.*

Shirts and Skins

The coach just hollered,
"Shirts and Skins!!" and I'm a Skin again.
I hate it when that happens, 'cause I'm 30 pounds too thin.
And since they turn the heat off after school in this old gym,
my goosebumps look like *moose* mumps
when I'm playin' for the Skins.

I'm cold as ice! (And standin' here half naked is the reason.)
Plus, I'm built just like a toothpick, so I take a lot of teasin'.
Therefore -
here's what *I* suggest to make the *best* of all this *freezin':*
let's just *forget* the basketball ...
and have a hockey season!

Future Archaeologist

I'll dig for hidden treasures
down through chasms deep and vast.
I'll bore through tons of muck
to find lost relics of the past.

I'll unearth ancient artifacts
thought not to have survived,
and find the grisly last remains
of creatures once alive.

I'll soon exhume a world of
wondrous scientific shockers -
my *gosh!* I love it when I hear,
"It's time to clean out lockers!"

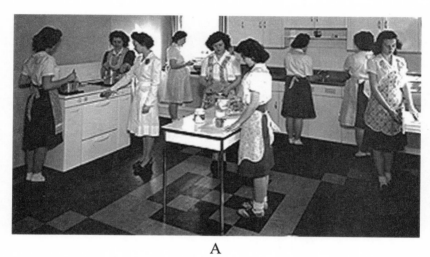

A

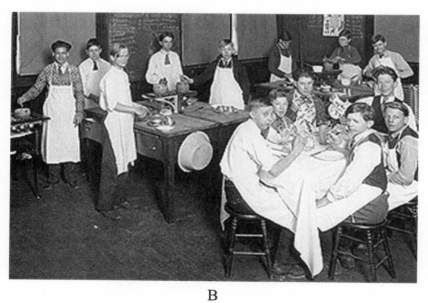

B

Home Ec

Let's make a few comparisons between these photographs.
If not for any other cause, then merely for the laughs.

In photo "A" we clearly witness classic "clean and neat",
while there in photo "B" things look confused, to say the least.

A also plainly demonstrates all hands are there to help,
while photo B is calling out, *"It's each man for himself!"*

The room in photo A is filled with
sweet scents worth the smellin',
while what the air in photo B is like, there ain't no tellin'.

The subjects there in A seem proudly sure of their success,
while those in B seem sure to make a cataclysmic mess.

And what you'd taste from photo A
would no doubt be delicious -
while that served up from B,
to say the least, would be suspicious.

Concerns from photo A are things like,
"Should I ice my cake?"
Concerns from B are things like,
"Hey! - Don't <u>block</u> the fire escape!"

Perhaps, I'm plain old prejudiced,
and shouldn't be that way ...
but, *you* can dine with whom you'd like -
my stomach votes for A.

I'm In, *You're* In!

While we shivered and froze
from our heads to our toes,
there in water that goose-bumped our skin,
not a' *one* of us guys
ever figured out why
it was oftentimes warmer near Ben.

Deer Unkl Bob

Deer Unkl Bob,

Tuday we had thu spelin be
jus thot id let yu no.
My ferst werd wuz a wethr werd
thay sed wud yu spel sno?

An so, i thot bout wut yu sed
to spel it lik it sounz.
But i dont thenk it werkt
cuz thay sed sory plez set doun.

Yu sed yud tech me math nex wek,
Mom herd yu wen yu sed it.
But she jus tode me
tel yur Unkl Bob to jus forgit it.

That Milestone of Manhood

There's a memory in place, that *I'd* like to erase -
just *forget* it, if I had the power.
T'was a task that was grueling, and often a cruel thing -
that milestone, called *7th grade showers*.
I remember it well: at the sound of the bell,
it was time to disrobe and discover.
The whole gang would strip down, then we'd all look around,
and pretend not to see one another.
If you brought in a note, from your mom that said, quote:
"My son *won't need* a shower today"
the teacher cared less, if you wound up embarrassed,
you took it all off *anyway*.
So, in there we stood, in our sheer manlihood -
bodies ranging from boys to grown men.
We all giggled like elves, then we dried off ourselves,
with a towel big enough for our shins.
Memories *feared* in some ways, and to this *very day*,
I've still got it so *clear* in my mind ...
when I stood in the buff - with the weak *and* the tough -
in a shower full of shiverin' behinds.

Shop

We're out here in shop, with the saws and the screws,
buildin' stuff, the Good Lord *alone* knows who can use.
Like a sheet metal scoop, or a 7-inch stool,
or aluminum dogs that take three days to cool.
Now, *could be* a plumb bob is somethin' of worth,
'cause we've made enough plumb bobs to plumb up the Earth.
I built *mom* a birdhouse - she hung it out back,
but the birds never come 'cause the yard's full of cats.
But *this* could be good ... it's a box with a lid.
Just the thing - to keep junk that I've made in here hid.

My Best Friend

My best friend said, "Hey, come *on,* man -
let's go behind the school!"
Which I, of course, did right away,
because my friend *was* cool.
And knowing just *how* cool he was,
I couldn't *wait* to see,
whatever in the world he had
to share back there with me.
But ...
instantly, *uncomfortably* - I found that I was dared,
and for the first time in our friendship
that guy had me scared.
I'm glad I *somehow* found the nerve
to turn and walk away,
and though we carried on as friends,
I learned a lot that day.

I didn't like the lesson,
but it made it plain to see -
the *only* person in the world
who *I* control ... is *me.*

Thank You, A-V Guys

Some called 'em nerds.
Some called 'em geeks.
Some called 'em high tech, A-V freaks.
But as for *me,* they'd make my week
by bringing those projectors!

And when, at times, a lightbulb croaked,
or when a film got stuck or broke,
those guys would pry and prod and poke
like homicide inspectors.

And soon enough, they'd have it fixed -
then, in the darkness, there we'd sit,
half rock-a-byed by mundane flicks
like: *Bees in Search of Nectar.*

So now, upon them, we should heap
a "world of thanks" for extra sleep,
and for the countless times they'd keep
us all from boring lectures.

The rumors are a-flyin' ...
"Johnny Jones loves Miss Ferree!"
She teaches typing classes,
and she's pretty as can be.
They say he works *real* slow,
so he can be the last to leave.
"Just so <u>those</u> two can be alone" -
(that's what *they* all believe).
But *they* don't know what's goin' on,
I know why Johnny lingers.
It's *not* because that boy's in love ...
John <u>still</u> types with two fingers!

Dale

Dale was big - Dale was strong ...
but now, *don't get me wrong!*
Playful, was Dale ... like a pup.
He would joke, and he'd smile,
and he *never* got riled,
so we nicknamed him *Sunny-Side Up.*
You could tell Dale was smart -
but in language-type arts,
he was pretty far back from the rest.
He would mix up his nouns,
and his phō-netic sounds,
and his writing was *really* a mess.
One day, in a class,
(that I doubt that he passed)
Dale was clowning, and had us in stitches.
The teacher erupted,
and said, "Keep it *up,* kid -
and *you'll* spend *your* days digging ditches!"
Well ...
if you see Dale *today,*
then you'll find right away,
that he's *still* not sure which witch that witch is.
But, my old buddy, Sunny,
sure rakes in the money,
with his crews who dig really *big* ditches.

The Dance

Paul: Go *ask* her, man!
Me: She'd just say, "No."
Paul: She *won't* say that.
Me: Shows what *you* know.
Paul: She looks <u>*real*</u> *nice!*
Me: I *know* she is.
Paul: Then *ask* her, man!
Me: Just mind your biz!
Paul: Brock! Brock! I *dare* ya!
Me: Yeah? Oh *yeah!?!*
Paul: I *dare* ya, man.
Me: I'm *going* ... **now!!**
Three minutes pass, my life is changed.
And then, I'm back with Paul again.
Me: I *did* it, man!!
Paul: Yo! Give me *five!*
Me: I didn't *die!*
Paul: Nope, still alive.
Me: Hey look! There's *Jan!*
Paul: I *know,* so *what?*
Me: You *love* her, man!
Paul: Well, maybe, but ...
Me: But *nothing,* Paul! It's *your* turn - *go!!*
Paul: You're *crazy,* man! ... She'd just say, "No."

Foreign Language

My first year, I took *Spanish* -
what do I remember? *"Si."*
I then signed up for *French,*
and am I glad *that's* over? *"Oui."*
This *German's* just as foreign,
which means now I'm "O for three".
But still, I'm learnin' *somethin'* ...
'cause it's all been *Greek* to me!

The Driver's Ed Devotion

As *we* roll forth into the world
within two tons of steel,
I ask advance forgiveness,
for my time behind the wheel.
And in my quest, to finally have
within my grasp a license,
I ask that thou not let me drive
like Indians after bison.

Be with thy good pedestrians,
and make them fleet of shoe.
Especially be with slow ones -
for they know not what they do.
Please spare from 'neath my wheels,
the dogs insane with ceaseless barking,
but most of all, dear Lord,
deliver me from parallel parking.

Sectional Victory!

One was thinkin' 'bout the dent he'd just put in the car.
One was thinkin' 'bout his brother, just sent off to war.
One was wonderin' if it showed his trunks weren't fittin' right,
and still *another* wondered where his father was that night.
Two were thinkin' 'bout their shovin' match before the game,
and how (because of *her*)
their friendship wouldn't be the same.
One was hopin' that he'd play (he hadn't played all year),
while *three* knew this could be the final game of their careers.
And *finally* ...
one was worried sick
about the math he'd been assigned -
so, *how* did those guys pull it off?

Your guess is good as mine.

Vocational Training

We laughed out *loud* at all those guys
who signed up for vocations -
and we'd *"Whoop!!"* when that bus hauled
'em off to some remote location.
So now ... I wonder why
we put up such a silly fuss -
'cause I'll be danged, if that *whole* gang
ain't got *better* jobs than *us!*

Halftime!

Those football guys were rough, it's true,
and other sports took toughness, too -
but the toughest crew *I* ever knew,
were those marching majorettes!

They practiced every day and night.
They'd twirl it left, then twirl it right,
then throw that thing clean out of sight,
and catch it right in step.

Then, on those *game* nights wet and cold,
that spinning spirit never slowed.
Inside those skintight suits of gold,
those girls would let it rip!

And likely now, a few are moms
who've passed to daughters their batons.
And after supper, on the lawn,
they practice pounding pep.

Drivin' Around

We're in my dad's car, and we're *drivin'* around.
We're headin' to wherever girls can be found,
'cause if we can find some, we'll show 'em the town.
And the best way to see it, *is drivin' around!*

We're in my dad's car and we're drivin' around.
We're rockin' and rollin' with AM for sound,
and our parents aren't here to say, *"Turn that noise down!!"*
while we're in my dad's car, and we're drivin' around.

We're in my dad's car, and we're drivin' around.
Let's drive up the hill - *turn around* - and drive *down!*
For two or three dollars, our freedom abounds,
when we're in my dad's car, and we're drivin' around.

We're in my dad's car, and we're drivin' around.
My license has lifted our feet from the ground.
And *bikes* are for kids who still *pedal* through town,
wishin' they were like *us,* 'cause *we're* drivin' around.

Worth It?

The distance? *Just 100 yards.*
Equipment? *Generations old.*
Positions? *Things like ends and guards.*
Conditions? *Wet. Or hot. Or cold.*
Investment? *Drills of endless length.*
The risk? *From bruise, to broken bone.*
The players? *Every size and strength.*
The reason? *Each would have his own.*
The pressure? *Fairly high at times.*
The coaches? *Fairly crazy.*
The plays? *Enough to ache your mind.*
Cheerleaders? *Most amazing!*
The humor? *Part of every day.*
It's topic? *I'm not saying.*
The games? *Like magic - cast our way.*
The pain? *One part of playing.*
Opponents? *Next to us, like pros.*
The thrill? *A leather ball.*
Our record? *Best left undisclosed.*
The memories? *More than worth it all.*

Playin' Along

Yeah, that's *me* rippin' through the ol' Homecomin' hoop.
The guys *shoved* me way up there in front of the group,
and I was all *proud as punch* to announce our arrival,
but let's just back up ... and talk *"Football Survival"*.

See ... *football* is where high school *guys* take a thumpin'
to get high school *girls* to think they're really somethin'.
And it didn't all matter that much if you'd lose,
just so long as you wound up with *some* kind of bruise,
'cause the girls, they would see it, and think you had nerve,
and you'd know that your purpose on Earth had been served.

So, *I* was keen enough playin' along with that bit -
just so long as it meant that I never got hit!
'Cause on a team known as *Bulldogs,*
I was more Golden Retriever ...
so, I figured I'd hide out at wide-out receiver.
Why? *Out there,* your job was just catchin' the ball -
and if *big* guys came *at* you, you just *dropped* it, that's all.

But - you dropped it with *style* ... or you dropped it with *flair.*
Main thing was you *dropped* it before they *got* there!
'Cause that could be bad, a for-real-life heart stopper.
Still, *I* didn't worry, 'cause I's an *expert* ball dropper.
But, *one* place I'd *keep* it, whence it had been thrown,
was when I found myself down in the end zone - *alone.*
'Cause when you caught it down *there,* you's feelin' so fine
and nobody'd *hit* you, 'cause you's past the *goal* line!
And the fans in the stands would jump up and they'd *scream!*
And the band would start playin' some star-spangled theme ...
and as far as my *football* career - that's about it.
I played *every* year, and I *never* got hit!

So, I never had bruises for girls to salute -
but, I *did* get a *paper* cut ... once from a hoop.

This Bus is Incredibly Hot!

This bus is incredibly hot! We're cookin' like beans in a pot!
I've never seen more kids, with sweat-drippin' foreheads,
this bus is *incredibly* hot!
Our shirts are stuck tight to our backs,
and we're crazy as bees in a sack.
(We'd be *less* bezerk, if the windows would work,
but they won't open more than a crack.)
And this bus is <u>incredibly</u> hot!!
How many more *miles* have we *got?!*
If it's *too* many more, then we'll all melt for *sure* -
just like bus-ridin' ...

buttery ...

blots.

110

Graduation Day

As I sit before family and friends in the stands,
I'm recalling the place where this journey began.
And I clearly see some with whom I used to play,
who were chosen by fate not to be here today.
I can also recall I felt timid, and small,
and I wondered if I'd ever grow up at all.
I was clumsy with scissors, and colored past lines,
and I found myself wrapped up in trouble at times.
Yet - I find myself *here.* How could such a thing be?
Could that same timid, clumsy kid really be me?
Well, of course, the kid could - that's how growing up goes!
But there *is* one small secret that made it all so.
And for it, I'm thankful to Almighty hands -
for I've *always* had family and friends in the stands.

... and so,

... and so, it comes to *this:*
though *schoolin'* days might lie behind us -
it's good, that now and then,
we look again at what defined us.

And when we *do,*
our thoughts might stray to sometimes senseless studies.
But, as for me? *From A to Z -*
the bunk was worth the buddies.